PROPHET YUNUS & THE BIG FISH IN THE SEA

FOR AGES 5 TO 9

BY THE SINCERE SEEKER KIDS COLLECTION

Once upon a time, there was a town of one hundred thousand people. They lived foolish lives, worshipping idols and believing these idols had powers. The people in the town had lots of money and lived proud lives. Then Allah, our Creator, sent one of his Prophets to the people to call and teach them to worship God alone without worshipping anyone or anything else and to follow God's Commandments and be good.

Allah sent Prophet Yunus (Jonah) PBUH to the town's people. Like all other Prophets of God, Prophet Yunus PBUH was a righteous man who worshipped God alone and helped those in need. Prophet Yunus PBUH instructed the people of the town to stop worshipping idols because idols are not God. Prophet Yunus PBUH showed them that the idols they worship cannot help nor harm them in any way and that God, alone, can help them.

But the people in this town did not listen to the Prophet God had sent. They told Prophet Yunus PBUH that their fathers and they had been worshipping these idols and were never harmed. They continued to worship idols and live disobedient lives. Some people in the town would make fun of Prophet Yunus PBUH. Prophet Yunus PBUH warned them that they would be punished if they continued to worship idols and how they lived. This threat did not scare or change the people in the town, and they continued to disbelieve, not taking God's message seriously. Some people even arrogantly laughed and challenged Prophet Yunus PBUH to bring on the punishment.

After some time of preaching the message of God to the people of the town, Prophet Yunus PBUH became frustrated and angry. He figured he would leave his people and go elsewhere to spread God's message to those who would listen and believe him. So, he left in anger without Allah telling him to go.

After Prophet Yunus PBUH left the town, the people noticed dark grey clouds forming in the sky. They started to worry. They stared at the skies in fear as a storm began to develop right before their eyes. *This is the warning of Prophet Yunus happening right in front of our eyes!* They cried, realizing the promised punishment was true.

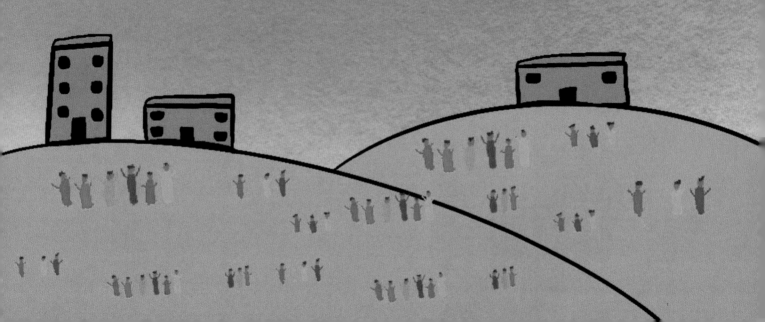

They understood that what Prophet Yunus PBUH had been teaching was true all along. The town felt bad for ignoring God's message and mistreating their Prophet. The entire village then believed in the message of God, destroyed their idols, and gathered in a mountain, crying and begging Allah for forgiveness and mercy.

Because the people finally believed in the message of God, stopped worshipping idols, and only worshipped God, God the Most-Merciful blessed them with a lot of money, food, animals, and more. This was the first time in human history that a whole town believed in the message of God. The people prayed for the return of Prophet Yunus PBUH so that he could teach and guide them to Allah, the Glorious, our Creator.

Meanwhile, Prophet Yunus PBUH, not knowing his people finally believed in the message of God, was on his way to board a small ship to travel to a nearby town to spread the message of Allah. Prophet Yunus PBUH boarded a small ship filled with goods with other passengers.

The small ship had sailed all day in calm waters with steady winds blowing at the sails. After the small boat had sailed for some distance, suddenly, at night, the small ship was caught in a storm that started to rock it back and forth, right and left, tossing and turning the small ship among the heavy tides. The small ship began to sink as the wind got wilder and wilder. Behind the small ship was a large fish-like whale following from behind.

The people on this ship knew they needed to lighten the heavy load, so they threw all their goods, baggage, and belongings into the sea so the ship wouldn't sink. But the small ship continued to rock back and forth, and they continued to sink slowly. Throwing everything overboard was not enough.

The sailors in the small ship decided they had no choice but to have someone jump off to lighten the load and save everyone else on the boat. The people on the ship wrongly believed that when the sea was violent, it was a sign that it was angry. Of course, that belief is not true. They drew lots to decide who would jump off the ship to save everyone else; whoever was chosen would need to jump off.

The lot was drawn, and Prophet Yunus's name was chosen. Prophet Yunus PBUH was known as an honorable and righteous man to the people on this ship, and they did not want to throw him into the angry sea. So, they decided to draw a second time and have someone else jump off. When they drew another name, Prophet Yunus's name was chosen once again. The sailors talked amongst themselves and decided to draw a third time, so someone else could jump off instead, but again, Prophet Yunus's name was chosen for the third time in a row.

Prophet Yunus PBUH understood that this was God's plan all along, for he had left his people and his mission without the permission of God. Prophet Yunus PBUH walked over to the edge of the small ship, looking down at the sea in the middle of the night. It was very dark, no moon was visible, and the stars were hidden behind a black fog. The passengers watched in horror as Prophet Yunus PBUH prepared to jump. He praised and mentioned Allah's Name and then jumped into the furious sea, immediately disappearing underneath the giant waves.

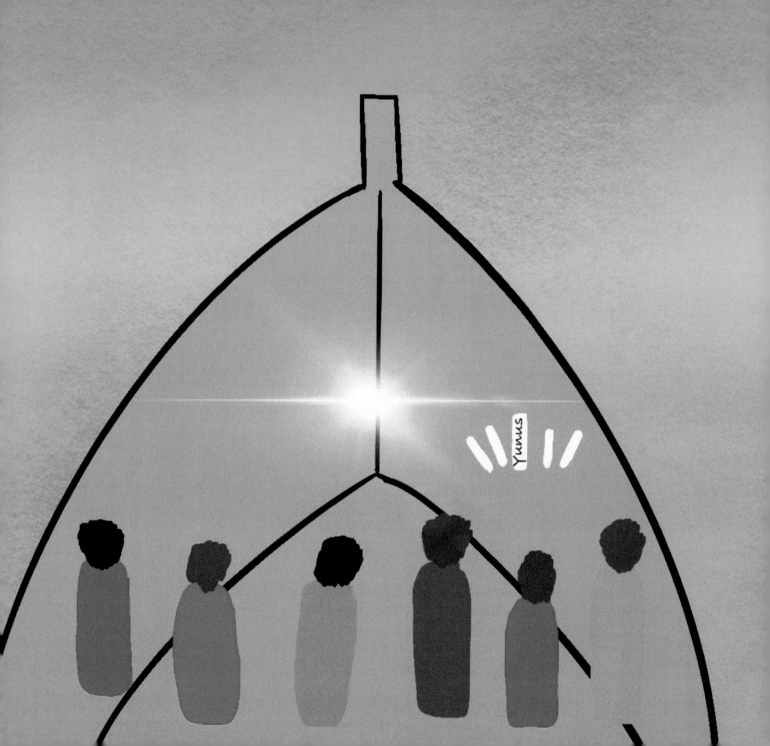

God then commanded the big fish, never seen before, to rush at Prophet Yunus PBUH and swallow him as he floated in the waves. The big fish opened its enormous mouth and swallowed Prophet Yunus PBUH. The big fish then swam to the bottom of the deep dark sea. He was imprisoned in the stomach of this big fish.

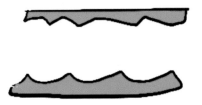

When Prophet Yunus PBUH awoke from unconsciousness: he thought he was dead. But then he saw that he could move his legs and was still alive. Prophet Yunus PBUH found himself in a tough place. He knew he was in the belly of a big fish, in the night's darkness at the bottom of the sea.

From the stomach of the big fish, Prophet Yunus PBUH heard pebbles and sea creatures worshipping and glorying God from the bottom of the sea in their unique ways. Prophet Yunus PBUH, filled with total despair, turned to Allah, prostrated before Him, and cried out, saying, *There is no deity except You; exalted are You. Indeed, I have been the wrongdoer.* After declaring the Greatness of Allah, he admitted his mistake and took responsibility for his actions. Prophet Yunus PBUH told God that he is praying and asking Him for his forgiveness from a place no one has ever called.

The Angels in the Heavens heard the cries of Prophet Yunus PBUH and recognized his voice. So, they asked Allah if that voice was the voice of Prophet Yunus PBUH, who always remembered God. God replied, *yes, that is my slave, Yunus.* The Angels pleaded to Allah to save Prophet Yunus PBUH. Prophet Yunus PBUH used to remember God when his life was easy, so God remembered Prophet Yunus PBUH when he was in a time of distress and needed God.

After days in the belly of the big fish, God commanded the creature to swim to shore to drop off Prophet Yunus PBUH on a remote Island. God had answered Prophet Yunus' prayers. The dua prayer that Prophet Yunus PBUH said is a very special dua. If anyone repeats this dua to Allah whenever they are in a difficult situation, God guarantees to answer their prayer every time. So, we should memorize and say this dua!

Prophet Yunus PBUH laid on the sand in the burning heat with no trees. When Prophet Yunus PBUH was placed aground, his skin was damaged from the acid of the belly's stomach, and he became sick. Prophet Yunus PBUH needed protection from the sun and wind. He prayed to God with the same prayers as before. Then God caused a tree to grow over Prophet Yunus PBUH. God blessed Prophet Yunus PBUH with food and shade to heal him.

continue spreading Allah's message, calling them to worship the one and only God without worshipping anyone else and to be good. So, he returned to his people, to the town of Nineveh. When he got there, he was pleasantly surprised to find that his people had never faced punishment and had changed for the better. The town had stopped worshipping idols and now worshipped Allah, the Glorious, alone, without anyone or anything else. They welcomed Prophet Yunus PBUH and were excited to see him again. Prophet Yunus PBUH was pleased to see his people submit to Allah.

We learn interesting lessons from the story of Prophet Yunus PBUH and his nation. Whenever you feel you're in a difficult position you want to get out of, you should recite this dua prayer, and Allah will find a way out for you just like he did for Prophet Yunus PBUH, who was in the darkest place one could be.

We learn we should remember God as much as possible because it will help us in many ways. We learn we need to apologize and ask God for forgiveness whenever we make a mistake. We also learn the importance of patience and its benefit in this story. Allah is always listening and there for us whenever we need him; he loves us very much, and we should love Him too 🖤.

The End.